Page 70

Page 110

tantalising cocktail and our selection of palate pleasers will make the task even more difficult!

We have divided the cocktails into four sections, indicating the time of day when they are most suitable to serve. Remember though, a cocktail can taste great at any time! Within the sections the cocktails are listed under their main ingredient, e.g. Tequila-based, Kahlua-based or Non alcoholic. All cocktails serve one person unless specified otherwise.

We have also advised in which glass the cocktail is traditionally served and the accompanying garnish, but the final choice is yours. Experiment with glassware, garnishes and cocktails to fit in with the mood of your gathering.

■ ■ ■

Produced by The Australian Women's Weekly
Home Library
Typeset by Photoset Computer Service Pty Ltd,
Sydney, Australia
Printed by Dai Nippon Co Ltd, Tokyo, Japan
Published by Australian Consolidated Press,
54 Park Street, Sydney
Distributed by Network Distribution Company,
54 Park Street, Sydney
Distributed in U.K. by Australian Consolidated Press (UK)
Ltd (0604) 760456. Distributed in New Zealand by Gordon
and Gotch (NZ) Ltd (09) 654 379. Distributed in Canada by
Whitecap Books Ltd (604) 980 9852. Distributed in South
Africa by Intermag (011) 493 3200.

■ ■ ■

■ ■ ■

Cocktail Guide

Includes index.
ISBN 0 949892 59 9.

1. COCKTAILS. (Series: Australian Women's Weekly Home
Library).

641. 874

ESSENTIAL EQUIPMENT

Many of the items may already be in your kitchen cupboard; the rest can easily be found in department stores or specialist shops.

All equipment by courtesy of Quality Cafe & Club Equipment, 53 William St, East Sydney. Blender from David Jones.

Blender: A very useful cocktail bar item. It should have several speed selections and be able to crush ice. The blender should be kept scrupulously clean. A Bamix can also be useful. **(1)**

Bottle opener: For beer bottles, any soft drink bottles or mixers without screw tops. **(2)**

Bowls: For olives, sugar, garnishes. **(3)**

Chopping board: On which to cut fruit. **(4)**

Corkscrew: To open wine or other corked bottles. **(5)**

Grater: For grating chocolate or nutmeg. **(6)**

Hawthorn strainer: A wire strainer which traps the ice but allows the liquid to pass through. It has an edge of rolled wire to prevent spillage. **(7)**

Ice bucket: For storing the ice to be used for drinks. **(8)**

Ice scoop: For getting ice for drinks. **(9)**

Juice extractor: Useful for making fresh fruit juice. **(10)**

Jug: Should have lips to hold back the ice, and be large enough to hold lots of ice. **(11)**

Knife: For chopping fruit. **(12)**

Measures: (Also called pourers, tots and jiggers), necessary to measure exact amount of ingredients. Most useful measures are 15ml and 30ml. **(13)**

Mixing glass: Used to stir cocktails and ensure the drink is served cold. A glass jug can be used. Should hold between 600ml to 1 litre and have lips.

Sealers: For mixer bottles and champagne bottles that have been opened and still have liquid left in them. **(14)**

Shaker: An American Shaker (consisting of two cones, one glass and one metal) is highly recommended, or a shaker with a built-in strainer. Make sure the lid is secure before shaking. **(15)**

Spoons: The long handled ones are the most useful for stirring. The handle should not be smooth as it may become slippery when wet; many of the spoons available have a spiral pattern on handle. **(16)**

Tongs: For fruit or ice. **(17)**

Tos or zester: To get zest from fruit peel. **(18)**

Other equipment you will need:
Stirrers or swizzle sticks, straws, toothpicks, serviettes, coasters and cloths.

MIXING A COCKTAIL

It takes years of practise to achieve a perfectly mixed cocktail, but with a few simple rules in mind you can create some sensational taste combinations.

Before mixing a drink have everything required close at hand and do as much as possible in advance. Use good quality products when mixing drinks and always follow recipes accurately. Measuring ingredients exactly is important if the drink is to have the right consistency. Prepare lots of fresh ice and have it ready for use, cut fruit into cubes and also check that your glassware is clean and in good order before guests arrive.

Serving food with cocktails will pace your guests' alcoholic intake and avoid mixing too many different spirits. The best drinks use one spirit as a base and have simple uncomplicated flavours. Use garnishes to add decoration and give an extra complimentary taste to the drink.

Some recipes may sound daunting if they mention too many different terms. Here are a few of the more common that may be encountered.

Float ingredients: A technique usually done after a cocktail has been made. A spoon is rested on the top of the drink and the liquid poured into its dish until the spoon is filled; the ingredients flow over it and onto the surface of the drink.

Muddling refers to the use of the back of the spoon (or special muddler) to mash aromatic ingredients together, (e.g. sugar cubes or mint leaves) to blend them and release the desired flavours and aromas.

Frosting is the technique where sugar or salt is used to coat the rim of a glass. To do this hold the glass upside-down, by the stem and rub a slice of lemon around the rim, then dip the glass into the sugar or salt and leave to dry. To achieve a coloured effect on the rim, place a little grenadine or coloured liqueur into a plate and coat the rim of the glass with it before dipping it in the sugar or salt.

Cocktails can be shaken, stirred, blended or built. These four methods of mixing are the most popular.
● To shake a cocktail is to mix it in a cocktail shaker by hand, making sure to fill the shaker three-quarters full with ice first. Pour the ingredients in on top of the ice. Cocktails that include ingredients such as egg whites, fresh juices and cream should be shaken for about 10 seconds, then strained into a cocktail glass.

● Stirred cocktails are mixed by stirring with ice in a mixing glass until cold and then are strained into a cocktail glass.

● Blended cocktails are mixed using an electric blender. Fresh fruit or fresh juices and alcohol are mixed well using this method. Add crushed ice last if recipe requires and blend long enough for it to be mixed with the liquid to reach the desired consistency; it should be smooth.

● Building a cocktail refers to mixing the ingredients in the glass which they will be served in. The ingredients are floated on top of each other and swizzle sticks can be placed in the glass to allow the ingredients to be mixed.

● A few more points to remember when mixing cocktails are:
 ● Always use good quality products.
 ● Juices should be at least 50 percent pure juice or they will water the cocktail down.
 ● After canned ingredients are opened, transfer them to clean bottles so they keep longer.

● Measurements of certain quantities are also useful to know when mixing drinks. The ones most often encountered are:
 ● a dash — 10 drops or ⅛ teaspoon
 ● 1 jigger — 1 pony (US) — 1oz — 30ml
 ● Miniature — 1.6oz — 50ml
 ● 1 wine glass (US) — 4oz — 25ml

Other cocktail terms:
Frappe: to serve a cocktail over finely crushed ice.
Flip: a drink made with eggs.
Mulls: hot wine punch.
Punch: mixed spirits or wines with spices, fruit juices and sugar. May be served hot or cold.

GLASSES

The glasses in which you serve your cocktails are every bit as important as the ingredients, the taste and the garnishes. Our recipes tell you in which glass the cocktail is traditionally served but the final choice is yours. Allow room for a generous amount of drink and garnishes.

Make sure the glass is completely free of any detergent or odour (if glasses are stored upside-down the air trapped in the bowl will become stale and affect the taste and smell of the drink); rinse these glasses before using.

If you have a large refrigerator or freezer it's a good idea to chill your glasses before using them. As well as being attractive, it keeps the drink chilled just that little bit longer.

Wash and rinse glasses in very hot water, then dry with one cloth and polish them with another.

Use real glass and not plastic glasses so as not to affect the taste of the drink. Remember too, that multicoloured designs on glasses tend to detract from the drink you are serving.

These glasses are the most used for cocktails:

Cocktail glass: A V shaped or triangular glass used for short, strong drinks. It should have a long stem to keep the cocktail chilled as long as possible. If the bowl of the glass is held in a warm hand, the hand becomes wet and the cocktail will lose its chill. Holds about 90ml. **(1)**

Champagne glass: Either a saucer or a flute shape. The long tapering flute **(2)** allows bubbles to rise in a continuous stream. Holds about 150ml. The saucer **(3)** is not as popular as it once was for champagne drinks as the bubbles disappear quickly, it is however still favoured for some cocktails such as the Margarita, Bartender and creamy drinks.

Highball: A tall straight-sided glass used mainly for long drinks with ice — anything from a lemonade or a Mai-Tai to a beer. Holds about 200-285ml. **(4)**

Old-fashioned: A tumbler with traditionally sloping sides used mainly for spirits with ice, short unstrained drinks or fruit juices. Holds about 120-125ml. **(5)**

Stemmed wine glasses: Available in a variety of shapes and sizes. Red wine is best served in a larger glass while white wine is suited to a smaller glass. Suitable for a range of exotic cocktails. Holds between 140-180ml. **(6)**

Brandy balloon: (not pictured) Designed so that the full aroma of the brandy can be savoured, but cocktails can look spectacular in these glasses. Should hold not more than 150ml.

ICE

Ice is used in nearly all cocktails so it is important to have clean, fresh cubes, blocks or crushed ice. Remember, a warm cocktail is, quite simply, undrinkable.

Well iced drinks are best because they have more body; the ice improves the texture by thickening the drink. It is important however to always add the ice first so it chills the liquid quickly and thoroughly and doesn't overflow the glass.

Prepare ice in the size and shape desired then place in the freezer for about 30 minutes to re-freeze it; melting ice is of little use.

Cubed ice can be prepared in freezer trays in many different sizes, and can be crushed easily. Crush ice cubes by wrapping them in a tea towel then hitting them on a wall or floor or with a hammer or rolling pin. Electric and hand-operated ice crushers are also available.

For ice cubes with a difference, place lemon wedges, fruit pieces or olive slices in water in ice tray. Allow to freeze, use in cocktails.

Tequila ~ based

BLUE MONDAY

30ML TEQUILA

30ML DRAMBUIE

30ML BLUE CURACAO

LEMONADE

ICE

Pour tequila, drambuie, curacao and ice into shaker, shake, then pour into serving glass. Top with lemonade.

Glass: 285ml highball.
Garnish: Lemon and orange slice and a cherry.
It is served in the afternoon.

RIGHT: Blue Monday.
Glass by Orrefors; ice bucket by Krosno

EYE OPENERS

Enticing drinks to awaken both you and your appetite. Choose from bubbling champagne delights, refreshingly fruity non-alcoholic mixtures or other spirited concoctions, then all that's left to do is to sit back and enjoy an unhurried breakfast as ceiling fans whirr overhead and the perfume of the blossoms fill the air. What a great thought to wake up to!

Brandy ~ based

MORNING GLORY

30ML BRANDY

15ML ORANGE CURACAO

15ML PURE LEMON JUICE

DASH ANGOSTURA BITTERS

DASH PERNOD

ICE

Pour all ingredients into shaker, shake, then strain into serving glass.

Glass: 90ml cocktail glass.
Garnish: Lemon twist.

RIGHT: Morning Glory

Brandy~based

CORPSE REVIVER

30ML BRANDY

15ML CALVADOS

15ML ROSSO VERMOUTH

ICE

Pour all ingredients into shaker, shake, then strain into serving glass.

Glass: 90ml cocktail glass.
Garnish: None.

RIGHT: Egg Nogg.
Glass by Nuutajarvi; pillow case by Sheridan

BELOW: Corpse Reviver.
Glass by Holmegaard

EGG NOGG

1 EGG

30ML BRANDY

30ML DARK RUM

90ML MILK

15ML SUGAR SYRUP

ICE

Pour sugar syrup, brandy, dark rum egg and ice into blender, blend, pour into serving glass then top up with milk. Stir.

Glass: 285ml highball.
Garnish: Nutmeg and a cherry.

Brandy ~ based

PRAIRIE OYSTER

1 EGG YOLK

SALT TO TASTE

PEPPER TO TASTE

DASH WORCESTERSHIRE SAUCE

2 DROPS TABASCO

30ML BRANDY
(OPTIONAL)

Pour ingredients into serving glass, one after the other. Preferably, do not stir, but swallow in one gulp. We cheated a little and stirred ours to make it look more desirable!

Glass: 90ml cocktail glass.
Garnish: None.

Champagne ~ based

MIMOSA

30ML FRESH ORANGE JUICE

10ML ORANGE CURACAO

CHILLED CHAMPAGNE

Pour curacao and juice into glass and top with champagne.

Glass: 140ml champagne flute.
Garnish: Orange twist.

LEFT: Prairie Oyster.

RIGHT: Mimosa.
Glass by Kosta Boda; bed linen by Sheridan

Beer ~ based

RED EYE

½ CHILLED BEER

½ TOMATO JUICE

Pour the ingredients together into beer glass.

Glass: Beer glass.
Garnish: None.

RIGHT: Perfect Love.
Glass by Iitala

BELOW: Red Eye.
Glass by Krosno

Vodka ~ based

PERFECT LOVE

30ML VODKA

15ML PARFAIT AMOUR

15ML MARASCHINO

ICE

Pour ingredients, one after the other, into serving glass filled with ice.

Glass: 140ml old-fashioned.
Garnish: Lemon twist.

Vodka ~ based

BLOODY MARY

30ML VODKA

120ML TOMATO JUICE

SALT OR CELERY SALT

PEPPER

DASH TABASCO SAUCE

DASH WORCESTERSHIRE SAUCE

DASH LEMON JUICE

ICE

Pour vodka, salt, pepper, tabasco sauce, Worcestershire sauce and lemon juice over ice in serving glass. Stir with swizzle stick. Add tomato juice and stir with swizzle stick.

Glass: 285ml highball.
Garnish: Lemon wedge and stick of crisp celery.

QUIET SUNDAY

30ML VODKA

15ML AMARETTO

120ML FRESH ORANGE JUICE

½ EGG WHITE

GRENADINE

ICE

Pour vodka, Amaretto, orange juice, egg white and ice into serving glass. Splash grenadine into glass last.

Glass: 285ml highball.
Garnish: Orange ring and cherry.

LEFT: Bloody Mary.
Glass by Iitala

RIGHT: Quiet Sunday.
Glass by Krosno

19

Vodka ~ based

BULLSHOT

30ML VODKA

120ML BEEF STOCK

7ML LEMON JUICE

DASH WORCESTERSHIRE SAUCE

PINCH CELERY SALT

PINCH PEPPER
TO TASTE

ICE

Pour all ingredients into shaker, shake, then strain into serving glass.

Glass: 285ml highball.
Garnish: Slice of lemon.

Sherry ~ based

SHERRY FLIP

60ML CREAM SHERRY

1 EGG

ICE

Pour all ingredients into blender, blend until smooth, then pour into serving glass.

Glass: 140ml wine goblet.
Garnish: Sprinkle of nutmeg.

LEFT: Bullshot.
Glass by Iitala; Hansa hand shower and hose "Five Stars"

RIGHT: Sherry Flip.
Glass by Krosno; bed linen by Sheridan

Bourbon ~ based

MINT JULEP

60ML BOURBON

5ML SUGAR SYRUP

5ML WATER

5 MINT LEAVES

ICE

Crush mint leaves in glass with sugar syrup and water to extract mint flavour. Add ice and bourbon. Stir for 30 seconds until glass frosts.

Glass: 180ml highball.
Garnish: Mint leaves.

Non ~ alcoholic

FRUIT FANTASY

120ML FRESH ORANGE JUICE

60ML PINEAPPLE JUICE

6 STRAWBERRIES

SMALL SLICE HONEYDEW MELON

SMALL SLICE ROCKMELON

ICE

Pour all ingredients into blender, blend until smooth, pour into serving glass.

Glass: 285ml highball.
Garnish: Fruit in season.

LEFT: Mint Julep.
Glass by Iitala

BELOW: Fruit Fantasy.
Glass by Orrefors

Non~alcoholic

PUSSYFOOT

60ML FRESH ORANGE JUICE

30ML PURE LEMON JUICE

30ML FRESH LIME JUICE

DASH GRENADINE

1 EGG YOLK

ICE

Pour all ingredients into shaker, shake, then pour into serving glass.

Glass: 285ml highball.
Garnish: Orange slice and cherry.

CINDERELLA

60ML ORANGE JUICE

60ML PINEAPPLE JUICE

60ML LEMON JUICE

ICE

Pour all ingredients into shaker, shake, then pour into serving glass.

Glass: 285ml highball.
Garnish: Fruit in season.

LEFT: Pussyfoot.
Glass by Orrefors

BELOW LEFT: Cinderella.
Glass by Iitala

BELOW RIGHT: Pom Pom.

POM POM

30ML PURE LEMON JUICE

½ EGG WHITE

5ML GRENADINE

CHILLED LEMONADE

ICE

Pour juice, egg white and grenadine into shaker, shake, then strain into serving glass. Top with lemonade, pouring slowly.

Glass: 285 highball.
Garnish: Lemon slice and cherry.

AFTERNOON DELIGHTS

During Prohibition in the 1920s adventurous drinkers began mixing bits and pieces together to disguise the taste of their poor quality liquor. We have followed the lead with gusto, although we don't need to cover the taste anymore, and today there is a tantalising range of cocktails, some just perfect for sipping in the lazy afternoon. Try an icy Frozen Daquiri, celebrate with a Rhett Butler, float away on a Barrier Reef, enjoy a Long Island Tea or introduce yourself to a Fluffy Duck.

Bacardi ~ based

BLOSSOM

45ML BACARDI

15ML FRESH ORANGE JUICE

15ML PURE LEMON JUICE

15ML SUGAR SYRUP

ICE

Pour all ingredients into shaker, shake, then strain into serving glass.

Glass: 140ml champagne saucer.
Garnish: Orange slice and a cherry.

LEFT: From left; Blossom, El Dorado (recipe over page).
Glasses by Holmegaard

Bacardi~based

EL DORADO

30ML BACARDI

30ML ADVOCAAT

30ML WHITE CREME DE CACAO

30ML COCONUT CREAM

ICE

Rub rim of glass with orange slice, dip rim into coconut to coat. Pour all ingredients into shaker, shake, strain into serving glass.

Glass: 285ml highball.
Garnish: Orange slices and cherries.

CASABLANCA

45ML BACARDI

90ML PINEAPPLE JUICE

30ML COCONUT CREAM

15ML GRENADINE

ICE

Pour all ingredients into blender, blend until smooth, then pour into a serving glass.

Glass: 285ml highball.
Garnish: Pineapple and a cherry.

RIGHT: Planter's Punch.
Glass by Iitala

BELOW: Casablanca.
Glass, jug by Iitala

PLANTER'S PUNCH

60ML BACARDI

30ML FRESH ORANGE JUICE

30ML FRESH LIME JUICE

5ML GRENADINE

DASH OF ANGOSTURA BITTERS

SODA WATER

ICE

Pour bacardi, juices, grenadine and bitters into serving glass filled with ice. Top with soda water and mix.

Glass: 285ml highball glass.
Garnish: Orange, lime and lemon slices and cherries.

Bacardi~based

BLUE HAWAII

30ML BACARDI

15ML AMARETTO

15ML BLUE CURACAO

15ML LIME CORDIAL

90ML PINEAPPLE JUICE

ICE

Pour all ingredients into shaker, shake, then pour into serving glass.

Glass: 285ml highball.
Garnish: Pineapple spear and a cherry.

PINA COLADA

30ML BACARDI

120ML PINEAPPLE JUICE

30ML COCONUT CREAM
(OR MALIBU)

15ML SUGAR SYRUP

ICE

Pour all ingredients into blender, blend until smooth, then pour into serving glass.

Glass: 285ml highball.
Garnish: Pineapple leaves and a cherry.

MAI-TAI

30ML BACARDI

15ML AMARETTO

15ML ORANGE CURACAO

15ML LEMON JUICE

15ML SUGAR SYRUP

30ML DARK RUM

LIME SHELL, SQUEEZED

ICE

Pour ingredients, one on top of the other, into serving glass filled with ice, stir gently with swizzle stick.

Glass: 285ml highball.
Garnish: Pineapple spear, leaves, cherry.

LEFT: From left: Blue Hawaii, Pina Colada.
Glass (left) by Iitala; glass (right) by Krosno

RIGHT: Mai Tai.
Glass by Iitala

31

Bacardi ~ based

BANANA COLADA

30ML BACARDI

30ML COCONUT CREAM

30ML SUGAR SYRUP

30ML FRESH CREAM

120ML PINEAPPLE JUICE

½ BANANA

ICE

Pour all ingredients into blender, blend, then pour into serving glass.

Glass: 300ml fancy.
Garnish: Banana, pineapple and mint leaves.

STRAWBERRY DAQUIRI

4 RIPE STRAWBERRIES

30ML BACARDI

30ML COINTREAU

30ML LEMON JUICE

ICE

Pour all ingredients into blender, blend, then strain into serving glass.

Glass: 140ml champagne saucer.
Garnish: Strawberry.

YELLOW BIRD

30ML BACARDI

22ML GALLIANO

22ML COINTREAU

22ML FRESH LIME JUICE

ICE

Pour all ingredients into shaker, shake, then pour into serving glass.

Glass: 180ml old-fashioned.
Garnish: Slice of lime in drink.

LEFT: From left: Strawberry Daquiri, Banana Colada.
Glass (left) by Holmegaard; glass (right) by Kosta Boda

BELOW: Yellow Bird.
Glass, jug from Market Imports, Melbourne

Bacardi~based

SARAH JANE

30ML BACARDI

15ML GRAND MARNIER

15ML APRICOT BRANDY

30ML ORANGE JUICE

30ML FRESH CREAM

7ML GALLIANO

ICE

Pour all ingredients into shaker, shake, then strain into serving glass.

Glass: 140ml champagne saucer.
Garnish: Chocolate flake, a strawberry.

FLUFFY DUCK

30ML BACARDI

30ML ADVOCAAT

LEMONADE

CREAM

ICE

Pour bacardi and advocaat into serving glass filled with ice and top with lemonade, mix well. Pour cream over a spoon so it overflows the spoon and floats on the surface of the drink.

Glass: 285ml highball.
Garnish: Strawberry.

FROZEN DAQUIRI

45ML BACARDI

30ML PURE LEMON JUICE

15ML SUGAR SYRUP

2 SCOOPS OF ICE

Pour all ingredients into blender, blend until smooth, then pour into serving glass.

Glass: 140ml champagne saucer.
Garnish: Lemon slice.

LEFT: From left: Sarah Jane, Fluffy Duck, Frozen Daquiri.
Glasses (left & right) by Krosno; glass (centre) by Iitala

Bacardi ~ based

BLUE HEAVEN

30ML BACARDI

15ML AMARETTO

15ML BLUE CURACAO

15ML FRESH LIME JUICE

75ML PINEAPPLE JUICE

ICE

Pour all ingredients into shaker, shake, then pour into serving glass.

Glass: 285ml highball.
Garnish: Pineapple piece, leaves and a cherry.

Vodka ~ based

SCREWDRIVER

60ML VODKA

60ML FRESH ORANGE JUICE

ICE

Pour ingredients, one after the other, into serving glass filled with ice.

Glass: 140ml old-fashioned.
Garnish: Orange slice.

HARVEY WALLBANGER

30ML VODKA

120ML ORANGE JUICE

15ML GALLIANO

ICE

Pour ingredients, one after the other, into serving glass filled with ice. Stir with a swizzle stick if desired.

Glass: 285ml highball.
Garnish: Orange slice and a cherry.

LEFT: Blue Heaven.
Glass by Krosno

Right: Screwdriver.
Glass from Market Imports, Melbourne

Vodka ~ based

LONG ISLAND TEA

30ML VODKA

30ML TEQUILA

30ML BACARDI

15ML COINTREAU

15ML PURE LEMON JUICE

15ML SUGAR SYRUP

30ML COLA

ICE

Pour all ingredients, one after the other, into serving glass filled with ice. Stir with a swizzle stick.

Glass: 285ml highball.
Garnish: Lemon twist and mint leaves.

RIGHT: From left: Salty Dog, Silver Sunset, Long Island Tea.
Glasses (left & right) by Iitala; glass (centre) by Orrefors

BELOW: Harvey Wallbanger (recipe previous page).
Glass by Iitala

SALTY DOG

45ML VODKA

120ML FRESH GRAPEFRUIT JUICE

ICE

Rub rim of glass with lemon slice then dip into salt, to coat the rim. Pour all ingredients, one after the other, into the salted glass filled with ice.

Glass: 285ml highball.
Garnish: Lemon twist.

SILVER SUNSET

30ML VODKA

15ML APRICOT BRANDY

15ML CAMPARI

90ML FRESH ORANGE JUICE

½ EGG WHITE

ICE

Pour all ingredients into shaker, shake, then pour into serving glass.

Glass: 285ml highball.
Garnish: Orange slice and cherry.

Tequila ~ based

VESUVIUS

30ML TEQUILA

120ML ORANGE JUICE

15ML CAMPARI

ICE

Pour ingredients, one after the other, over ice into serving glass.

Glass: 285ml highball.
Garnish: Orange spiral.

ACAPULCO

30ML TEQUILA

30ML TIA MARIA

30ML DARK RUM

30ML PINEAPPLE JUICE

30ML COCONUT CREAM

ICE

Pour all ingredients into shaker, shake, then pour into serving glass.

Glass: 285ml highball.
Garnish: Pineapple slice, leaves and a cherry.

VIVA MEXICO

30ML TEQUILA

22ML WHITE CREME DE CACAO

22ML MIDORI MELON LIQUEUR

30ML PINEAPPLE JUICE

3ML ORANGE JUICE

ICE

Pour all ingredients into shaker, shake, then pour into serving glass.

Glass: 285ml highball.
Garnish: Slice of orange and a cherry.

RIGHT: From left: Vesuvius, Acapulco, Viva Mexico.
Glass (left) by Iitala; glass (centre) by Krosno; glass (right) by Orrefors

Tequila ~ based

BRAVE BULL

30ML TEQUILA

30ML KAHLUA

ICE

Pour ingredients, one after the other, into serving glass filled with ice, stir if desired.

Glass: 185ml old-fashioned.
Garnish: None.

TEQUILA SUNRISE

30ML TEQUILA

120ML ORANGE JUICE

7ML GRENADINE

ICE

Pour ingredients, one after the other, over ice in serving glass. Drop grenadine through centre of cocktail.

Glass: 285ml highball.
Garnish: Orange slice and a red cherry.

RIGHT: Tequila Sunrise.
Glass by Nuutajarvi

BELOW: Brave Bull
Glass from Market Imports, Melbourne

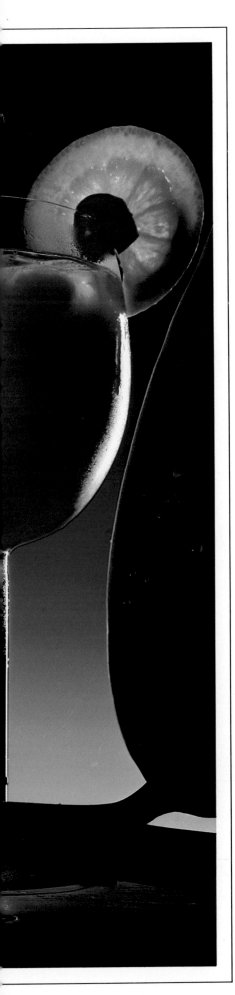

Brandy ~ based

BRANDY HIGHBALL

30ML BRANDY

DASH ANGOSTURA BITTERS

CHILLED SODA WATER
(OR GINGER ALE)

ICE

Coat inside of glass with bitters. Top with soda water or ginger ale.

Glass: 285ml highball.
Garnish: Lemon spiral.

SOUTHERLY BUSTER

30ML BRANDY

15ML DRY VERMOUTH

15ML LIME CORDIAL

DRY GINGER ALE

ICE

Pour brandy, dry vermouth and lime cordial into serving glass filled with ice. Top with dry ginger ale.

Glass: 285ml highball.
Garnish: Lemon slice.

BELOW: From left: Brandy Highball, Southerly Buster.
Glasses by Iitala

Rum~based

COCONUT BREEZE

30ML DARK RUM

30ML PINEAPPLE JUICE

30ML COCONUT CREAM

7ML MARASCHINO

7ML AMARETTO

ICE

Pour all ingredients into shaker, shake, then pour into serving glass.

Glass: 140ml champagne saucer.
Garnish: Sprinkle with grated coconut.

LOVE IN THE AFTERNOON

30ML DARK RUM

30ML FRESH ORANGE JUICE

30ML COCONUT CREAM

15ML SUGAR SYRUP

15ML FRESH CREAM

5 STRAWBERRIES

ICE

Pour all ingredients into blender, blend until smooth, then strain into serving glass.

Glass: 180ml old-fashioned.
Garnish: Chocolate flake and a strawberry.

Beer~based

BLACK VELVET

½ STOUT BEER

½ CHAMPAGNE

Pour all ingredients into serving glass.
Stir if desired.

Glass: Champagne flute.
Garnish: None.

RIGHT: Black Velvet.
Glass by Holmegaard

*BELOW: From left: Coconut Breeze,
Love in the Afternoon.*
Glasses by Krosno

Gin~based

BLUE LAGOON

30ML GIN OR VODKA

120ML LEMONADE

30ML BLUE CURACAO

ICE

Pour ingredients, one after the other, into serving glass filled with ice, stir with swizzle stick if desired.

Glass: 285ml highball.
Garnish: Orange slice and cherry.

NEGRONI

22ML GIN

22ML ROSSO VERMOUTH

22ML CAMPARI

SODA WATER
(OPTIONAL)

ICE

Pour ingredients, one after the other, into serving glass filled with ice.

Glass: 285ml highball.
Garnish: Orange slice.

RAFFLES SINGAPORE SLING

DASH ANGOSTURA BITTERS

30ML GIN

15ML TRIPLE SEC

15ML BENEDICTINE

15ML CHERRY BRANDY

15ML FRESH LIME JUICE

30ML PINEAPPLE JUICE

30ML FRESH ORANGE JUICE

ICE

Pour all ingredients, one after the other, into serving glass filled with ice, stir gently with swizzle stick.

Glass: 285ml highball.
Garnish: Orange slice and a cherry.

RIGHT: From left: Blue Lagoon, Negroni.
Glasses by Iitala

FAR RIGHT: Raffles Singapore Sling.
Glass by Krosno

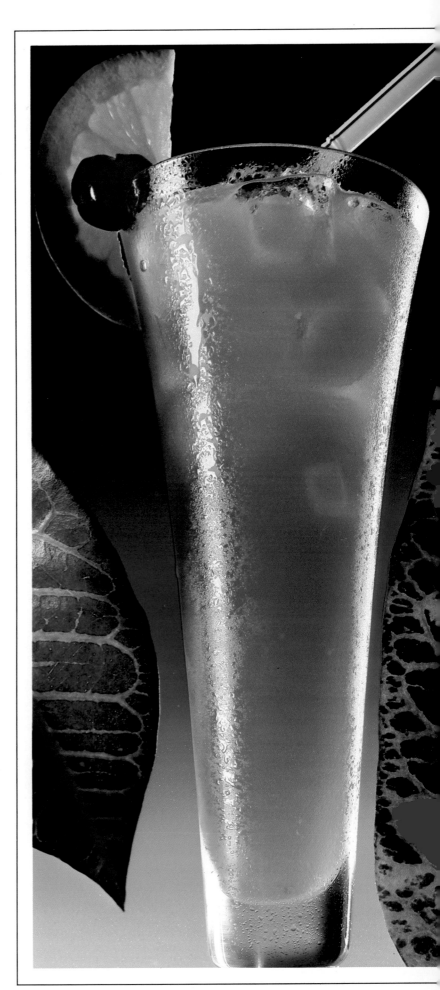

Gin~based

CARIBBEAN SUNSET

30ML GIN

30ML BANANA LIQUEUR

30ML BLUE CURACAO

30ML PURE LEMON JUICE

30ML FRESH CREAM

DASH OF GRENADINE

ICE

Pour gin, banana liqueur, blue curacao, lemon juice and cream into shaker with ice, shake, strain into serving glass. Add grenadine.

Glass: 300ml cocktail glass.
Garnish: Fruit in season.

BARRIER REEF

60ML GIN

30ML COINTREAU

DASH ANGOSTURA BITTERS

2 SCOOPS VANILLA ICE-CREAM

DASH BLUE CURACAO

ICE

Pour all ingredients into shaker, shake, then pour into serving glass.

Glass: 285ml highball.
Garnish: Pineapple slice and leaves.

BLUE BAYOU

30ML GIN

15ML GALLIANO

15ML DRY VERMOUTH

15ML BLUE CURACAO

LEMONADE

ICE

Pour gin, Galliano, vermouth and curacao into shaker, shake, then pour into serving glass. Top with lemonade.

Glass: 285ml highball.
Garnish: Lemon wheel and mint leaves.

LEFT: Caribbean Sunset.
Glass by Holmegaard

RIGHT: From left: Barrier Reef, Blue Bayou.
Glass (left) by Kosta Boda; glass (right) by Orrefors

Gin ~ based

SOUTH PACIFIC

30ML GIN

15ML GALLIANO

LEMONADE

15ML BLUE CURACAO

ICE

Pour gin and Galliano into serving glass filled with ice, top with lemonade. Splash blue curacao through the drink; it will sink to the bottom of the drink.

Glass: 285ml highball.
Garnish: Lemon slice.

MOON RIVER

30ML GIN

30ML APRICOT BRANDY

30ML COINTREAU

15ML GALLIANO

15ML FRESH LIME JUICE

ICE

Pour all ingredients into shaker, shake, then pour into serving glass.

Glass: 285ml highball.
Garnish: Orange or lemon slice and a cherry.

LEFT: From left: South Pacific, Moon River.
Glass (left) by Orrefors; glass (right) by Iitala

RIGHT: Crazy Horse (recipe over page).
Glass is "Provence" by Kosta Boda

Whisky ~ based

CRAZY HORSE

30ML SCOTCH WHISKY

15ML STRAWBERRY LIQUEUR

15ML CREME DE BANANE

CHILLED CHAMPAGNE

ICE

Pour scotch whisky, strawberry liqueur, crème de banane and ice into shaker, shake, then strain into serving glass. Top with champagne.

Glass: **180ml** champagne flute.
Garnish: Orange and lime slices, a strawberry and mint leaves.

OLD-FASHIONED

60ML PREFERRED SCOTCH WHISKY

30ML SODA WATER

1 SUGAR CUBE

ANGOSTURA BITTERS

ICE

Soak a sugar cube with bitters and place into serving glass. Cover cube with soda water, crush and mix to dissolve cube. Add ice, stir, then add scotch whisky.

Glass: **180ml** old-fashioned.
Garnish: Orange and lemon slices and a cherry.

Wine ~ based

SANGRIA

1 BOTTLE RED WINE

30ML COINTREAU

30ML BACARDI

30ML BRANDY

½ CUP SUGAR

ICE

Pour ingredients into a large jug filled with ice, stir well until combined, then pour into serving glass.

Glass: **140ml** wine goblet.
Garnish: Orange, lemon and strawberry pieces.

SPRITZER

½ CHILLED WHITE WINE

½ CHILLED SODA WATER

Pour together into serving glass.

Glass: 180ml wine goblet.
Garnish: None.

LEFT: Old-Fashioned
Glass is "Intermezzo Blue" by Orrefors

ABOVE: Sangria.

RIGHT: Spritzer.
Glass by Nuutajarvi; vase is "Caramba" by
Kosta Boda

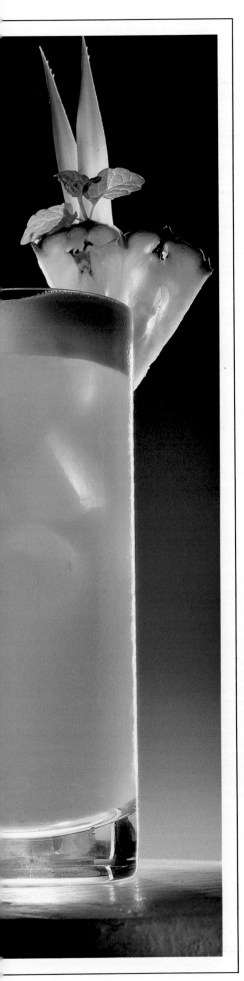

Galliano ~ based

ROCKMELON DREAM

30ML GALLIANO

22ML MARASCHINO

30ML FRESH ORANGE JUICE

30ML FRESH CREAM

3 SCOOPS ROCKMELON

ICE

Pour all ingredients into blender, blend until smooth, then pour into serving glass.

Glass: 140ml champagne glass.
Garnish: Rockmelon balls.

BOSSA NOVA

30ML GALLIANO

30ML BACARDI

15ML APRICOT BRANDY

15ML PURE LEMON JUICE

30ML PINEAPPLE JUICE

DASH EGG WHITE

ICE

Pour all ingredients into shaker, shake, then pour into serving glass.

Glass: 285ml highball.
Garnish: Pineapple slice, leaves, mint.

LEFT: From left: Rockmelon Dream, Bossa Nova.
Glass (left) by Holmegaard; glass (right) by Orrefors

BELOW: Peach Marnier (recipe overpage).
Glass by Iitala

Grand Marnier ~ based

PEACH MARNIER

30ML GRAND MARNIER

30ML DARK RUM

30ML PINEAPPLE JUICE

30ML SUGAR SYRUP

2 TINNED PEACH HALVES

ICE

Pour all ingredients into blender, blend until smooth, then pour into serving glass.

Glass: 180ml old-fashioned.
Garnish: Peach slice and a cherry.

Banana Liqueur ~ based

WHITE GOLD

30ML BANANA LIQUEUR

30ML GALLIANO

30ML PINEAPPLE JUICE

30ML APRICOT NECTAR

½ EGG WHITE

ICE

Pour all ingredients into blender, blend until smooth, then pour into serving glass half-filled with ice.

Glass: 285ml highball.
Garnish: Cherry and pineapple piece.

Curacao ~ based

RHETT BUTLER

30ML ORANGE CURACAO

30ML SOUTHERN COMFORT

15ML PURE LEMON JUICE

15ML FRESH LIME JUICE

SODA WATER

ICE

Pour curacao, Southern Comfort, juices and ice into shaker, shake, then pour into serving glass. Top with soda water.

Glass: 285ml highball.
Garnish: Orange slice and mint leaves.

Malibu ~ based

FRENCH BLUE

30ML MALIBU

15ML STRAWBERRY LIQUEUR

¼ BANANA

15ML BLUE CURACAO

ICE

Pour all ingredients into blender, blend until smooth, then pour into serving glass.

Glass: 140ml champagne saucer.
Garnish: Strawberries and banana slices.

RIGHT: Rhett Butler.
Glass by Orrefors

FAR RIGHT: From left: French Blue, White Gold.
Glass (left) by Orrefors; glass (right) by Kosta Boda

Southern Comfort~based

KELLY'S COMFORT

30ML SOUTHERN COMFORT

30ML BAILEYS IRISH CREAM

60ML MILK

4 STRAWBERRIES

15ML SUGAR SYRUP

ICE

Pour all ingredients into blender, blend until smooth, then pour into serving glass.

Glass: 285ml highball.
Garnish: Strawberry.

PERNOD POLYNESIAN

30ML SOUTHERN COMFORT

15ML PERNOD

60ML ORANGE AND MANGO JUICE

30ML FRESH CREAM

15ML BLUE CURACAO

ICE

Pour Southern Comfort, Pernod, juice, cream and ice into shaker, shake, then pour into serving glass. Drop blue curacao through drink; it will sink to the bottom of the drink.

Glass: 285ml highball.
Garnish: Orange slice and cherry.

FAR RIGHT: El Burro.
Glass by Nuutajarvi

BELOW: From left: Kelly's Comfort, Pernod Polynesian.
Glass (left) by Iitala; glass (right) by Krosno

Kahlúa Bavarian Coffee
1 oz. Kahlúa
½ oz. peppermint schnapps
Hot coffee
Whipped cream
Add Kahlúa and schnapps to coffee. Top with whipped cream. Garnish with shaved chocolate, if desired.

Kahlúa & Hot Chocolate
1½ oz. Kahlúa
Hot chocolate
Whipped cream *or* marshmallows
Prepare hot chocolate according to your favorite recipe. Add Kahlúa. Stir. Top with whipped cream or marshmallows.
For a minty variation, try 1 oz. Kahlúa and ½ oz. peppermint schnapps.

Kahlúa Kioki Coffee
1 oz. Kahlúa
½ oz. brandy
Hot coffee
Whipped cream
Add Kahlúa and brandy to coffee. Top with whipped cream.

Kahlúa Mexican Coffee
Use Kahlua Kioki Coffee recipe, substituting ½ oz. tequila for brandy. Dust with cocoa powder, if desired.

Kahlúa & Coffee
1½ oz. Kahlúa
Hot coffee
Cream, plain or whipped
Add Kahlúa to coffee. Stir in cream or top with whipped cream, if desired.

Kahlúa Parisian Coffee
½ oz. Kahlúa
½ oz. Grand Marnier
1 oz. cognac *or* brandy
Hot coffee
Whipped cream
Pour first 3 ingredients into a steaming cup of coffee. Top with whipped cream. Garnish with shaved chocolate or orange peel, if desired.

Kahlúa Hot Spiced Apple Cider
1½ oz. Kahlúa
8 oz. hot cider *or* apple juice
Cinnamon stick
Pour Kahlúa into hot cider or apple juice. Stir with cinnamon stick. A cozy variation: add 1 oz. apple schnapps.

Kahlúa Irish Coffee
1 oz. Kahlúa
1 oz. Irish whiskey
Hot coffee
Whipped cream
Add Kahlúa and Irish whiskey to coffee and top with whipped cream.

Kahlúa Black Russian Pie

1 cup cream-filled chocolate sandwich cookie crumbs (about 14 cookies)
2 Tbsp. butter, melted
24 large marshmallows
½ cup cold milk
⅛ tsp. salt
⅓ cup Kahlúa
1 cup whipping cream
Optional: Whipped cream and chocolate curls

To make crust, combine cookie crumbs and butter. Press firmly over bottom and sides of 9 in. pie pan. Freeze until firm. Melt marshmallows with milk and salt over hot water. Cool until mixture mounds on a spoon. Stir in Kahlúa. Whip cream until stiff peaks form; fold into mixture. Chill until mixture ripples when lightly stirred (about 30 min.). Turn into chilled cookie crust. Re-freeze until firm. Garnish, if desired. Serves 8.

Kahlúa White Russian Pie

Kahlúa Browned Butter Crust
1 envelope unflavored gelatin
¼ cup cold water
3 large eggs, separated
7 Tbsp. granulated sugar
¼ cup Kahlúa
3 Tbsp. vodka
½ cup whipping cream
Kahlúa Cream Topping
Optional: Chocolate curls

Prepare Kahlúa Browned Butter Crust; chill. Soften gelatin in cold water; let stand 5 min. Dissolve over hot water. Beat egg yolks with *4 Tbsp.* sugar until thick and lemon-colored. Gradually beat in gelatin mixture. Stir in Kahlúa and vodka. Cool, stirring occasionally, until mixture thickens slightly. Beat egg whites until frothy;

then, one at a time, beat in *3 Tbsp.* sugar until stiff peaks form. Fold into Kahlúa-gelatin mixture. Whip cream until stiff peaks form; fold in. Chill mixture a few min. until it mounds on a spoon. Turn *half* into chilled crust. Sprinkle with reserved crust mixture. Top with remaining filling; chill several hrs. or overnight. Before serving, swirl Kahlúa Cream Topping over pie. Garnish, if desired. Serves 8.

Kahlúa Browned Butter Crust:
In saucepan, heat ½ cup butter until lightly browned. Remove from heat. Add 1 Tbsp. Kahlúa. Stir in 2½ cups finely crushed packaged shortbread cookies and 2 Tbsp. granulated sugar; blend well. Reserve ½ cup for pie's center. Press remaining crumbs firmly over bottom and sides of buttered 9 in. pie pan; chill.

Kahlúa Cream Topping:
Whip 1 cup whipping cream with 2 Tbsp. Kahlúa until stiff peaks form.

Kahlúa Mousse

1 lb. dark sweet chocolate, cut in pieces
3 oz. butter, cut in pieces
½ cup sifted powdered sugar
3 eggs, separated
¼ cup Kahlúa
1 tsp. instant coffee powder
2 cups whipping cream
Optional: Whipped cream

In top of double boiler, melt chocolate and butter over simmering water. In large bowl, combine sugar, yolks, Kahlúa and coffee powder. Blend in chocolate mixture. Whip cream until stiff peaks

form; fold into Kahlúa-chocolate mixture. Beat egg whites until soft peaks form; fold into mixture. Spoon into serving bowl or dessert glasses. Refrigerate 4 hrs. or overnight. Garnish, if desired. Serves 6-10.

Kahlúa Chocolate Nut Squares

1¼ cups sifted all-purpose flour
¾ tsp. baking powder
½ tsp. salt
½ cup butter, softened
¾ cup brown sugar, packed
1 large egg
¼ cup *plus* 1 Tbsp. Kahlúa
1 cup semi-sweet chocolate pieces
⅓ cup chopped walnuts or pecans
Brown Butter Icing
Optional: Nut halves

Grease a 7 x 11 in. baking pan. Preheat oven 350°F. Resift flour with baking powder and salt. Cream butter and sugar; beat in egg. Stir in ¼ cup Kahlúa, then flour mixture; blend well. Fold in chocolate pieces and nuts. Spread evenly in prepared pan. Bake 30 min., or until top springs back when touched lightly in center. Do not overbake. Remove from oven, cool in pan 15 min., then brush top with 1 Tbsp. Kahlúa. When fully cooled, spread with Brown Butter Icing. When icing is set, cut into bars, about 2 x 1½ in. Garnish, if desired. Makes 2 doz.

Brown Butter Icing:
In saucepan, heat 2 Tbsp. butter until lightly browned. Remove from heat. Add 1 Tbsp. Kahlúa, 2 tsp. milk *or* cream and 1⅓ cups sifted powdered sugar; beat until smooth.

Kahlua~based

EL BURRO

15ML KAHLUA
15ML DARK RUM
30ML COCONUT CREAM
30ML FRESH CREAM
½ BANANA
ICE

Pour all ingredients into blender, blend until smooth, then pour into serving glass.

Glass: 180ml old-fashioned.
Garnish: Banana slice and mint leaves.

Kahlua ~ based

B52

30ML KAHLUA

30ML BAILEYS IRISH CREAM

30ML COINTREAU

ICE

Pour ingredients, one after the other, into serving glass filled with ice and stir with swizzle stick.

Glass: 180ml old-fashioned.
Garnish: None.

WHITE RUSSIAN

30ML KAHLUA

30ML VODKA

30ML FRESH CREAM

ICE

Pour ingredients, one after the other, over ice in serving glass and stir with swizzle stick.

Glass: 180ml old-fashioned.
Garnish: None.

Tia Maria ~ based

LAZY DAZE

30ML TIA MARIA

15ML VODKA

30ML GREEN CREME DE MENTHE

LEMONADE

FRESH CREAM

ICE

Pour Tia Maria, vodka, and crème de menthe into serving glass filled with ice. Top with lemonade, stir. Pour cream over a spoon so it overflows and floats on the surface.

Glass: 285ml highball.
Garnish: Cherry and mint leaves.

LEFT: B52.
Glass by Krosno

ABOVE: White Russian.
Glass by Iitala

RIGHT: Lazy Daze.
Glass by Holmegaard

Ouzo~based

JELLY BEAN

30ML OUZO

15ML BLUE CURACAO

15ML GRENADINE

LEMONADE

ICE

Pour ouzo, blue curacao and grenadine into serving glass filled with ice. Top with lemonade.

Glass: 285ml highball.
Garnish: Jelly bean.

HOT APHRODITE

22ML OUZO

30ML VANDERMINT

22ML GREEN CREME DE MENTHE

22ML FRESH CREAM

ICE

Pour all ingredients into shaker, shake, then strain into serving glass.

Glass: 140ml champagne saucer.
Garnish: Black grapes and mint leaves.

LEFT: Jelly Bean.
Glass by Orrefors

BELOW: Hot Aphrodite.
Glass by Holmegaard

ABOVE: Touch of Zam (recipe over page).
Glass by Orrefors

Sambuca ~ based

TOUCH OF ZAM

22ML SAMBUCA

22ML BENEDICTINE

22ML GLAYVA

30ML ORANGE JUICE

15ML FRESH LEMON JUICE

ICE

Pour all ingredients into shaker, shake, then strain into serving glass.

Glass: 140ml champagne saucer.
Garnish: Orange and lemon slices.

Apricot Brandy ~ based

CHAMPAGNE CHARLIE

15ML APRICOT BRANDY

CHILLED CHAMPAGNE

Pour apricot brandy into serving glass. Top with champagne.

Glass: 180ml champagne flute.
Garnish: Orange slice.

Pernod ~ based

DEATH IN THE AFTERNOON

22ML PERNOD

CHILLED CHAMPAGNE

Pour Pernod into serving glass. Top with chilled champagne.

Glass: 180ml champagne flute.
Garnish: None.

Midori ~ based

ISLAND AFFAIR

30ML MIDORI MELON LIQUEUR

15ML COINTREAU

15ML BLUE CURACAO

120ML ORANGE AND MANGO
JUICE

30ML COCONUT CREAM

ICE

Pour ingredients, one after the other, into serving glass filled with ice. Stir with swizzle stick if desired.

Glass: 285ml highball.
Garnish: Slice of pineapple and a cherry.

LEFT: From left: Champagne Charlie, Death in the Afternoon.
Glass (left) by Holmegaard; glass (right) by Kosta Boda

Advocaat ~ based

DIZZY BLONDE

60ML ADVOCAAT

30ML PERNOD

LEMONADE

ICE

Pour advocaat and Pernod into serving glass filled with ice. Top with lemonade.

Glass: 285ml highball.
Garnish: Red cherry.

FALLEN ANGEL

30ML ADVOCAAT

30ML CHERRY ADVOCAAT

LEMONADE

ICE

Pour advocaat and cherry advocaat into serving glass filled with ice. Top with lemonade. Stir well.

Glass: 285ml highball.
Garnish: Red cherry.

LEFT: Island Affair (recipe previous page).
Glass by Orrefors

RIGHT: From left: Dizzy Blonde, Fallen Angel.
Glass (left) by Krosno; glass (right) by Holmegaard

Non ~ alcoholic

PASSION

1 BANANA
60ML PINEAPPLE JUICE
60ML ORANGE AND MANGO JUICE
3 TEASPOONS PASSIONFRUIT PULP
ICE

Pour all ingredients into blender, blend until smooth, then pour into serving glass.

Glass: 285ml highball.
Garnish: Banana and pineapple slices.

CAIRNS COOLER

60ML PINEAPPLE JUICE
60ML FRESH ORANGE JUICE
30ML COCONUT CREAM
15ML SUGAR SYRUP
ICE

Pour ingredients, one after the other, into serving glass filled with ice.

Glass: 285ml highball.
Garnish: Pineapple slice, leaves and a cherry.

SURFERS PARADISE

30ML FRESH LIME JUICE
2 DASHES ANGOSTURA BITTERS
LEMONADE
ICE

Pour lime juice and bitters, one after the other, over ice in serving glass. Top with lemonade.

Glass: 285ml highball.
Garnish: Orange slice.

SHIRLEY TEMPLE

30ML GRENADINE
LEMONADE
FRESH CREAM
ICE

Pour ingredients, one after the other, over ice in serving glass. Top with lemonade and mix well. Float fresh cream on top.

Glass: 285ml highball.
Garnish: Red cherry.

RIGHT: From left: Surfers Paradise, Shirley Temple.
Glass (left) by Kosta Boda; glass (right) by Krosno

BELOW: From left: Passion, Cairns Cooler.
Glasses by Iitala

PRE-DINNER DRINKS

Cocktails are the perfect lead-in to dinner. Traditionally the martini — sweet, dry or medium — has occupied pride of place, but the choice is a varied one. Opt for a sparkling Kir Royale, a brandy-based Sidecar, a smooth Whisky Sour or a zesty Margarita to get your evening off to a tasty start.

Ouzo ~ based

BLUE NEGLIGEE

22ML OUZO

22ML PARFAIT AMOUR

22ML GREEN CHARTREUSE

ICE

Pour all ingredients into shaker, shake, then strain into serving glass.

Glass: 90ml cocktail glass.
Garnish: Red cherry.

Campari ~ based

AMERICANO

30ML CAMPARI

30ML ROSSO VERMOUTH

SODA WATER

ICE

Pour campari then vermouth into serving glass filled with ice. Top with soda water, stir if desired.

Glass: 185ml old-fashioned.
Garnish: Orange wheel and lemon spiral.

Bourbon ~ based

FRENCH 95

15ML BOURBON

15ML PURE LEMON JUICE

15ML SUGAR SYRUP

CHILLED CHAMPAGNE

ICE

Pour bourbon, lemon juice and sugar syrup into shaker with ice, shake, then strain into serving glass. Top with champagne.

Glass: 140ml champagne flute.
Garnish: Lemon spiral.

RIGHT: From left: French 95, Americano, Blue Negligee.
Glasses by Orrefors

Vodka ~ based

VODKA MARTINI

45ML VODKA

15ML DRY VERMOUTH

ICE

Pour all ingredients into mixing glass filled with ice, stir, then strain into serving glass.

Glass: 90ml cocktail glass.
Garnish: Lemon twist.

KAMIKAZE

30ML VODKA

30ML COINTREAU

30ML LEMON JUICE

5ML LIME CORDIAL

ICE

Pour all ingredients into shaker, shake, then strain into serving glass.

Glass: 140ml champagne saucer.
Garnish: Red cocktail onion.

LEFT: Vodka Martini.
Glass, pitcher by Orrefors; stirrer by Krosno

RIGHT: Kamikaze.
Glass by Orrefors

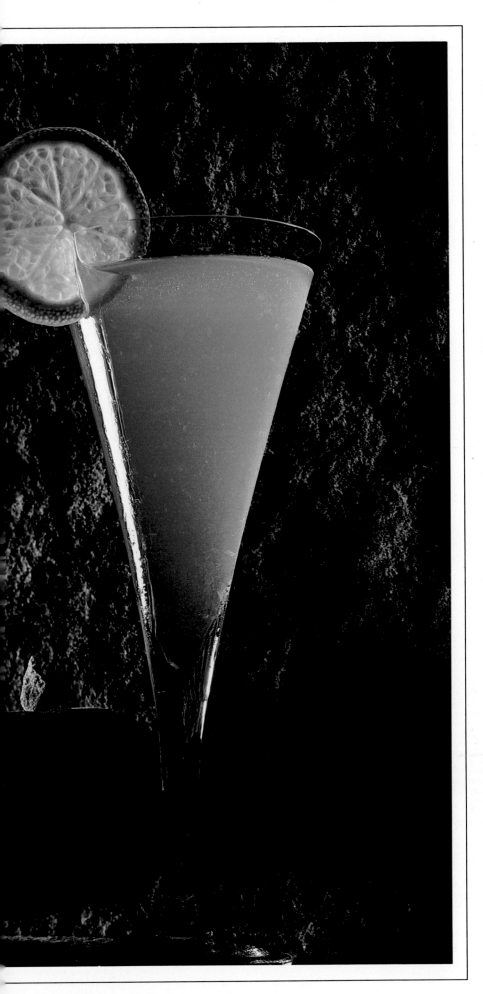

Vodka ~ based

GREEN FANTASY

30ML VODKA
30ML DRY VERMOUTH
20ML MIDORI MELON LIQUEUR
10ML FRESH LIME JUICE
ICE

Pour all ingredients into shaker, shake, then strain into serving glass.

Glass: 90ml cocktail glass.
Garnish: Lime wheel, strawberry and mint leaves.

BLUE BALALAIKA

22ML VODKA
22ML COINTREAU
BLUE CURACAO
22ML PURE LEMON JUICE
ICE

Pour all ingredients into shaker, shake, then strain into serving glass.

Glass: 90ml cocktail glass.
Garnish: Lemon twist.

LEFT: From left: Blue Balalaika, Green Fantasy.
Glasses by Krosno

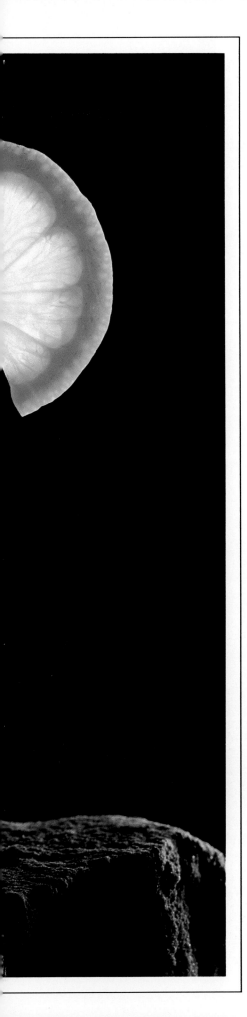

Midori ~ based

JAPANESE SLIPPER

30ML MIDORI MELON LIQUEUR

30ML VODKA

30ML PURE LEMON JUICE

ICE

Pour all ingredients into shaker, shake, then strain into serving glass.

Glass: 140ml champagne saucer.
Garnish: Lemon slice.

Brandy ~ based

STINGER

45ML BRANDY

15ML WHITE CREME DE MENTHE

ICE

Pour all ingredients into mixing glass filled with ice, stir, then strain into serving glass.

Glass: 90ml cocktail glass.
Garnish: None.

BRANDY CRUSTA

30ML BRANDY

15ML MARASCHINO

30ML FRESH ORANGE JUICE

DASH ANGOSTURA BITTERS

Rub rim of serving glass with orange slice then dip into sugar to coat rim. Pour all ingredients into shaker, shake, then strain into serving glass.

Glass: 140ml champagne flute.
Garnish: Orange slice and cherry.

LEFT: Japanese Slipper.
Glass by Orrefors

*LEFT: From left:
Brandy Crusta,
Stinger (recipes
previous page).
Glass (left) by Kosta
Boda; glass (right) by
Orrefors*

79

Brandy~based

RIGHT: Between the Sheets.
Glass is "Eclair" by Holmegaard

BELOW: Sidecar.
Glass by Krosno

SIDECAR

30ML BRANDY

30ML COINTREAU

30ML PURE LEMON JUICE

ICE

Pour all ingredients into shaker, shake, then strain into serving glass.

Glass: 90ml cocktail glass.
Garnish: Lemon twist.

BETWEEN THE SHEETS

30ML BRANDY

30ML BACARDI

30ML COINTREAU

7ML LEMON JUICE

ICE

Pour all ingredients into shaker, shake, then strain into serving glass.

Glass: 140ml champagne saucer.
Garnish: Lemon twist.

Champagne ~ based

CHAMPAGNE COCKTAIL

1 SUGAR CUBE

6 DROPS ANGOSTURA BITTERS

15ML BRANDY OR COGNAC

CHILLED CHAMPAGNE

Soak sugar cube with bitters and drop into champagne flute, pour brandy or cognac on top of bitters, then fill with chilled champagne.

Glass: 140ml champagne flute.
Garnish: Orange slice.

BELLINI

½ FRESH PEACH

CHILLED CHAMPAGNE

Blend ½ peach into purée in blender, spoon into serving glass and top with chilled champagne.

Glass: 140ml champagne flute.
Garnish: Slice of fresh peach.

RITZ FIZZ

CHILLED CHAMPAGNE

DASH AMARETTO

DASH BLUE CURACAO

DASH STRAINED PURE LEMON JUICE

Pour Amaretto, juice and blue curacao into serving glass and top with chilled champagne.

Glass: 140ml champagne flute.
Garnish: Float a rose petal on the surface if desired.

LEFT: Chamgagne Cocktail.
Flute by Orrefors

RIGHT: Bellini.
Flute by Orrefors

FAR RIGHT: From left: Ritz Fizz, Sweet Martini (recipe overpage).
Glass (left) is "Provence" by Kosta Boda; glass (right) is "Intermezzo Blue" by Orrefors

Gin~based

SWEET MARTINI

45ML GIN

15ML ROSSO VERMOUTH

ICE

Pour all ingredients into mixing glass filled with ice, stir and strain into serving glass.

Glass: 90ml cocktail glass.
Garnish: Red cherry.

MARTINI

45ML GIN

15ML DRY VERMOUTH

ICE

Pour all ingredients into mixing glass filled with ice, stir and strain into serving glass.

Glass: 90ml cocktail glass.
Garnish: Olive or lemon twist.

RIGHT: Martini.
Glasses are "Victoria" by Orrefors; jug by Orrefors; stirrer by Krosno

Gin ~ based

GIBSON

60ML GIN

5ML DRY VERMOUTH

ICE

Pour all ingredients into mixing glass filled with ice, stir, then strain into serving glass.

Glass: 90ml cocktail glass.
Garnish: White cocktail onion.

AFTER ONE

22ML GIN

22ML GALLIANO

22ML BIANCO VERMOUTH

22ML CAMPARI

ICE

Pour all ingredients into mixing glass filled with ice, stir, then strain into serving glass.

Glass: 90ml cocktail glass.
Garnish: Red cherry and an orange twist.

GIMLET

45ML GIN

15ML LIME CORDIAL

ICE

Pour all ingredients into mixing glass filled with ice, stir, then strain into serving glass.

Glass: 90ml cocktail glass.
Garnish: Lemon twist.

LEFT: From left: Gimlet, After One, Gibson.
Tumbler is "Intermezzo Blue" by Orrefors; glasses (right & centre) are "Monte Carlo" by Holmegaard

Gin~based

PERFECT LADY

30ML GIN

15ML PEACH BRANDY

15ML LEMON JUICE

1 EGG WHITE

ICE

Pour all ingredients into shaker filled with ice, shake, then strain into serving glass.

Glass: 90ml champagne saucer.
Garnish: Peach slice.

BARTENDER

22ML GIN

22ML MEDIUM SHERRY

22ML ROSSO VERMOUTH

22ML DRY VERMOUTH

7ML GRAND MARNIER

ICE

Pour all ingredients into mixing glass filled with ice, stir, then strain into serving glass.

Glass: 140ml champagne saucer.
Garnish: Orange spiral and a cherry.

LEFT: Perfect Lady.
Glass by Krosno

BELOW: Bartender.
Glass by Orrefors

Gin ~ based

GIN & IT

30ML GIN

30ML BIANCO VERMOUTH

ICE

Pour all ingredients into mixing glass filled with ice, stir, then strain into serving glass.

Glass: 90ml cocktail glass.
Garnish: Red cherry.

VICTORIA

30ML GIN

30ML DRY VERMOUTH

22ML APRICOT BRANDY

5ML GRENADINE

ICE

Pour gin, dry vermouth and apricot brandy into mixing glass filled with ice, stir, then strain into serving glass. Drop grenadine through the centre of the drink.

Glass: 90ml cocktail glass.
Garnish: Stemmed red cherry.

THE FILBY

30ML GIN

15ML AMARETTO

15ML CAMPARI

15ML DRY VERMOUTH

ICE

Pour all ingredients into mixing glass filled with ice, stir, then strain into serving glass.

Glass: 90ml cocktail glass.
Garnish: Orange twist.

PINK GIN

45ML GIN

1 DASH ANGOSTURA BITTERS

30ML WATER
(OPTIONAL)

Coat inside of wine goblet with bitters, add chilled gin then cold water if desired.

Glass: 90ml cocktail glass.
Garnish: None.

BLUE RIBAND

30ML GIN

30ML WHITE CURACAO

15ML BLUE CURACAO

ICE

Pour all ingredients into mixing glass filled with ice, stir, then strain into serving glass.

Glass: 90ml cocktail glass.
Garnish: Orange twist and a cherry.

EVERGREEN

30ML GIN

15ML DRY VERMOUTH

15ML MIDORI MELON LIQUEUR

7ML BLUE CURACAO

ICE

Pour, gin, dry vermouth and Midori melon liqueur into mixing glass filled with ice, stir, then strain into serving glass. Drop blue curacao through the centre of the drink.

Glass: 90ml cocktail glass.
Garnish: Red cherry.

LEFT: From left: Gin & It, Victoria, The Filby.
Glass (left) is "Eclair" by Holmegaard; glasses (centre & right) by Orrefors

*LEFT: From left: Pink
Gin, Blue Riband,
Evergreen (recipes
previous page).
Glasses by Orrefors*

93

RIGHT: From left: French 75, Dunk Cocktail, Clover Club (recipes over page).
Glasses by Orrefors

Gin ~ based

FRENCH 75

15ML GIN

15ML PURE LEMON JUICE

15ML SUGAR SYRUP

CHILLED CHAMPAGNE

ICE

Pour gin, lemon juice, sugar syrup and ice into shaker, shake, then strain into serving glass. Top with champagne.

Glass: 140ml champagne flute.
Garnish: Lemon twist and a red cherry.

CLOVER CLUB

60ML GIN

15ML LEMON JUICE

15ML GRENADINE

½ EGG WHITE

ICE

Pour all ingredients into shaker, shake, then strain into serving glass.

Glass: 140ml champagne saucer.
Garnish: Lemon slices.

DUNK COCKTAIL

60ML GIN

30ML DRY VERMOUTH

22ML GALLIANO

10ML BLUE CURACAO

ICE

Pour all ingredients into mixing glass filled with ice, stir, then strain into serving glass.

Glass: 140ml champagne saucer.
Garnish: Red cherry.

Bacardi ~ based

BACARDI COCKTAIL

30ML BACARDI

15ML PURE LEMON JUICE

7ML GRENADINE

EGG WHITE
(OPTIONAL)

ICE

Pour all ingredients into shaker, shake, then strain into serving glass.

Glass: 90ml cocktail glass.
Garnish: Red cherry.

DAQUIRI

45ML BACARDI

30ML PURE LEMON JUICE

15ML SUGAR SYRUP

EGG WHITE
(OPTIONAL)

ICE

Pour all ingredients into shaker, shake, then strain into serving glass.

Glass: 140ml champagne saucer.
Garnish: Lemon slice.

APRICOT LADY

30ML BACARDI

30ML APRICOT BRANDY

15ML ORANGE CURACAO

15ML FRESH LIME JUICE

½ EGG WHITE

ICE

Pour all ingredients into blender, blend until smooth, then pour into serving glass.

Glass: 185ml old-fashioned.
Garnish: Orange slice and a red cherry.

BANANA DAQUIRI

30ML BACARDI

30ML PURE LEMON JUICE

30ML SUGAR SYRUP

¾ FRESH BANANA

ICE

Pour all ingredients into blender, blend until smooth, then pour into serving glass.

Glass: 140ml champagne saucer.
Garnish: Slice of banana and mint leaves.

LEFT: From left: Bacardi Cocktail, Daquiri.
Glass (left) by Orrefors; glass (right) by Krosno

LEFT: From left:
Apricot Lady,
Banana Daquiri
(recipes previous
page).
Glasses by Holmegaard

99

Tequila ~ based

30ML TEQUILA

30ML LENA BANANA LIQUEUR

7ML BLUE CURACAO

ICE

Pour tequila and banana liqueur into mixing glass filled with ice, stir, then strain into serving glass. Drop blue curacao through centre of cocktail to achieve a two tone effect. The blue curacao will sink because it is heavier than the other ingredients.

Glass: 90ml cocktail glass.
Garnish: Lime wheel.

MARGARITA

30ML TEQUILA

15ML PURE LEMON JUICE

30ML TRIPLE SEC OR COINTREAU

EGG WHITE
(OPTIONAL)

ICE

Rub rim of glass with lemon slice, then dip in salt to coat rim. Pour all ingredients into shaker, shake, then strain into serving glass.

Glass: 140ml champagne saucer.
Garnish: Lemon slice.

LEFT: Olé.
Glass is "Goldline" by Kosta Boda

BELOW: Margarita.
Glass is "Goldline" by Kosta Boda

Whisky ~ based

WHISKY SOUR

45ML WHISKY
(PREFERRED BRAND)

30ML FRESH LEMON JUICE

15ML SUGAR SYRUP

½ EGG WHITE
(OPTIONAL)

Pour all ingredients into shaker, shake, then strain into serving glass.

Glass: 180ml wine-stemmed goblet.
Garnish: Red cherry at bottom of glass, lemon slice on side of glass.

RIGHT: Whisky Sour.
Glass by Orrefors

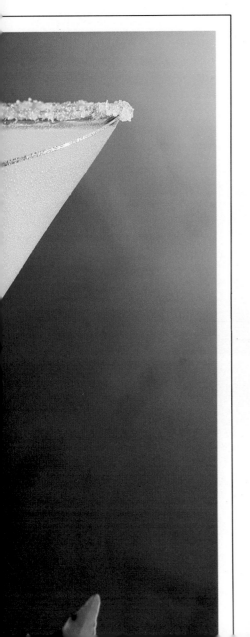

Whisky ~ based

BLOOD & SAND

30ML SCOTCH WHISKY

30ML ROSSO VERMOUTH

30ML CHERRY BRANDY

30ML ORANGE JUICE

ICE

Pour all ingredients into shaker, shake, then strain into serving glass.

Glass: 140ml champagne saucer.
Garnish: Orange spiral and a cherry.

ROB ROY

30ML SCOTCH WHISKY

30ML ROSSO VERMOUTH

DASH ANGOSTURA BITTERS

ICE

Pour all ingredients into mixing glass filled with ice, stir, then strain into serving glass.

Glass: 90ml cocktail glass.
Garnish: Red cherry.

LEFT: Blood & Sand.
Glass by Orrefors

RIGHT: Rob Roy.
Jug, stirrer by Holmegaard

Whiskey~based

MANHATTAN

45ML RYE WHISKEY
15ML ROSSO VERMOUTH
DASH ANGOSTURA BITTERS

Pour all ingredients into mixing glass filled with ice, stir, then strain into serving glass.

Glass: 90ml cocktail glass.
Garnish: Red cherry.

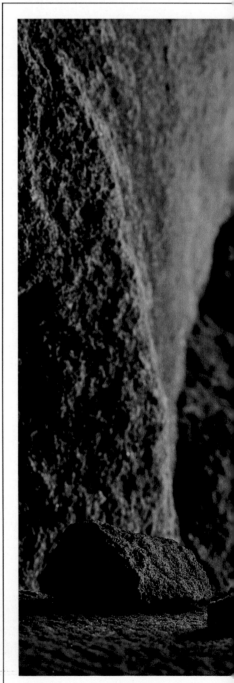

Galliano~based

GALLIANO MIST

30ML GALLIANO

LEMON PEEL SLICE
(SHAKEN WITH INGREDIENTS)

ICE

Pour all ingredients into shaker, shake,
then pour into serving glass.

Glass: 180ml old-fashioned.
Garnish: None.

LEFT: Manhattan.
Glass is "Vision" by Orrefors

BELOW: Galliano Mist.
Glass by Iitala

Grand Marnier ~ based

GLOOM CHASER

30ML GRAND MARNIER

30ML ORANGE CURACAO

30ML LEMON JUICE

7ML GRENADINE

ICE

Pour all ingredients into shaker, shake, then strain into serving glass.

Glass: 140ml champagne saucer.
Garnish: Orange twist.

Lena Banana Liqueur ~ based

THE RIPPER

22ML LENA BANANA LIQUEUR

22ML PEACHTREE LIQUEUR

15ML PURE LEMON JUICE

22ML DRY VERMOUTH

7ML BLUE CURACAO

ICE

Pour Lena banana liqueur, Peachtree liqueur, juice and dry vermouth into shaker with ice, shake, then strain into serving glass. Drop blue curacao through centre of drink.

Glass: 90ml cocktail glass.
Garnish: Lemon wheel and mint leaves.

Cognac ~ based

HAPPY WORLD

15ML COGNAC

30ML COINTREAU

30ML ORANGE JUICE

15ML BANANA LIQUEUR

Pour all ingredients into shaker, shake, then strain into serving glass.

Glass: 140ml champagne saucer.
Garnish: Orange slice and a cherry.

RIGHT: From left: Gloom Chaser, The Ripper, Happy World.
Glasses are from the Ken Done Collection by Kosta Boda

Crème de Cassis~based

KIR ROYALE

5ML CREME DE CASSIS

CHILLED CHAMPAGNE

Pour crème de cassis into serving glass and top with champagne.

Glass: 140ml champagne flute.
Garnish: None.

KIR

15ML CREME DE CASSIS

CHILLED DRY WHITE WINE

Pour crème de cassis into serving glass and top with white wine.

Glass: 140ml wine goblet.
Garnish: None.

LEFT: Kir Royale.
Glass is "Monte Carlo" by Holmegaard

RIGHT: Kir.
Carafe is "Intermezzo" by Orrefors; glass is
"Provence" by Kosta Boda

NIGHTCAPS

Drift off with these sublime nightcaps. Spice up the coffee with some Irish whiskey and a cloud of cream or dispense with it all together and try a Hot Buttered Rum, a Scotch Mist or a Grand Marnier Fireball. Sweet dreams.

Grand Marnier ~ based

GRAND MARNIER FIREBALL

30ML GRAND MARNIER

30ML COGNAC

ORANGE WEDGE

Pour ingredients into a warm brandy balloon, ignite and add orange wedge. Let flame for about 15 seconds, then extinguish and inhale fumes while glass is cooling.

Glass: 285ml brandy balloon.
Garnish: None.

Amaretto ~ based

P.S. I LOVE YOU

30ML AMARETTO

30ML KAHLUA

30ML BAILEYS IRISH CREAM

ICE

Pour all ingredients, one on top of the other, over ice in serving glass and stir with a swizzle stick.

Glass: 185ml old-fashioned.
Garnish: Sprinkles of nutmeg.

RIGHT: Grand Marnier Fireball.

BELOW: P.S. I Love You.
Glass by Krosno; compact, lipstick by Estee Lauder (below).

Whisky ~ based

45ML SCOTCH WHISKY

22ML DRAMBUIE

ICE

Pour ingredients, one on top of the other, over ice in serving glass.

Glass: 180ml old-fashioned.
Garnish: Lemon twist.

RIGHT: Hot Toddy.
Glass by Orrefors

BELOW: Rusty Nail.
Glass by Orrefors

60ML SCOTCH WHISKY
(OR ANY PREFERRED SPIRIT OR
LIQUEUR)

1 TEASPOON HONEY OR
BROWN SUGAR

BOILING WATER

Pour spirit or liqueur into serving glass, add honey or sugar then top with boiling water.

Glass: 140ml wine goblet.
Garnish: Lemon slice studded with cloves, a cinnamon stick and a sprinkle of nutmeg.

Whisky~based

BLUE BLAZER

60ML SCOTCH WHISKY
60ML BOILING WATER
15ML SUGAR SYRUP

Pour scotch into silver goblet, and boiling water and sugar syrup into another goblet. Ignite scotch and gently pour on top of boiling water. Pour back and forth between goblets to mix.

Glasses: Two silver goblets or heatproof glasses.
Garnish: Lemon twist.

SCOTCH MIST

30ML SCOTCH WHISKY
TWIST OF LEMON
ICE

Pour all ingredients into shaker, shake, then pour into serving glass.

Glass: 180ml old-fashioned.
Garnish: None.

LEFT: Blue Blazer.
Glasses by Krosno

BELOW: Scotch Mist.
Glass by Orrefors

116

Rum ~ based

HOT BUTTERED RUM

1 SMALL SLICE BUTTER

1 TEASPOON BROWN SUGAR

CINNAMON

NUTMEG

VANILLA ESSENCE

30ML DARK RUM

BOILING WATER

Mix butter, brown sugar, cinnamon, nutmeg and vanilla essence until creamed. Place one teaspoon into a serving glass, pour dark rum and boiling water into serving glass and mix well.

Glass: 180ml stemmed wine goblet.
Garnish: None.

HOT EGG NOGG

15ML DARK RUM

15ML BRANDY

7ML SUGAR SYRUP

1 EGG

HOT MILK

Pour rum, brandy, sugar syrup and egg into blender, blend for about 30 seconds then pour into serving glass. Top with hot milk and mix well.

Glass: 285ml highball.
Garnish: Nutmeg.

LEFT: Hot Buttered Rum.
Glass by Krosno

RIGHT: Hot Egg Nogg.
Glass by Krosno

Vodka ~ based

BLACK RUSSIAN

30ML VODKA

30ML KAHLUA

COLA TOP UP
(OPTIONAL)

ICE

Place a scoop of crushed ice in serving glass. Pour in vodka then Kahlua. Top up with cola if desired.

Glass: 185ml old-fashioned.
Garnish: None.

RIGHT: Glühwein.
Glass by Orrefors

BELOW: Black Russian.
Glass by Krosno

Wine ~ based

GLÜHWEIN

1 BOTTLE RED WINE

3 TABLESPOONS SUGAR

2 SLICES LEMON

2 SLICES ORANGE

1 CINNAMON STICK

Warm all ingredients in a saucepan until very hot. Do not boil. Serve in a heated goblet.

Glass: 140ml wine goblet.
Garnish: None.

Irish Whiskey ~ based

IRISH COFFEE

30ML IRISH WHISKEY

120ML HOT BLACK COFFEE

1 TEASPOON BROWN SUGAR

FRESH CREAM

Put sugar into the bottom of serving glass and cover with Irish whiskey. Top with coffee and mix well. Float cold cream on the surface by pouring it into a teaspoon and letting it overflow on to the surface of the drink.

Glass: Irish coffee glass.
Garnish: Grated chocolate.

*RIGHT: Irish
Coffee (recipe
previous page).
Glass by Krosno*

GARNISHES

*Choose fruit that is firm, unblemished
and has a good colour. Wash fruit just before use.*

To make a spiral: Using a vegetable peeler, peel off a 10-15cm length strip of peel (about ½cm wide) in a continuous spiral from the selected fruit. Do not cut into the bitter white pith.

To make a knot: Using a vegetable peeler, remove thin strips of peel from selected fruit. Gently tie each strip into a knot and drop knot into drink.

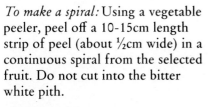

*Left: Lemon spirals. Below left:
Lemon, lime and orange strips of
peel and knots. Below right:
Lemon wheels and slices with
nicks in the peel. Bottom
right: Lemon wheel
twisted with a cherry
on a toothpick.*
Garnishes photographed
by Justine Kerrigan.
Prepared by
Jon Allen.

Fruit slices: Place fruit on its side and cut crosswise segments with a knife. To make the slices more decorative, first score the skin of the fruit with a vegetable peeler, pulling it from top to bottom across the skin to expose the pith. This will cause indents in the skin, the fruit can then be cut.

Whole or half slices can also be twisted using a cocktail stick or toothpick to secure them. Different coloured fruit slices can also be twisted together and balanced on the glass rim.

Strawberries: Choose firm ripe strawberries with nice green leafed tops. Cut strawberry in half lengthwise. For more elaborate decoration, make several cuts lengthways into the strawberry's flesh to form a fan.

Bananas: Choose firm unblemished fruit and prepare just before serving. Cut unpeeled bananas into slices, dip in lemon juice to prevent discolouration. Make a cut into centre of slice and balance on glass rim. Pair with a cherry or other colourful fruit.

Left: Strawberry fan. Right: Strawberry, pineapple leaves and lemon piece on a toothpick.

Melons: Use a melon scoop to remove balls from different types of melons. Spear balls on a toothpick and use as a garnish.

Fresh coconut: Crack coconut shell with hammer. Pare off thin peelings of coconut with a sharp knife. These will curl up and can be used on top of the drink, or on glass rim. Alternatively, grate coconut flesh and sprinkle on top of drink.

Pineapple: Leaves from head of pineapple can be sliced in the centre at the bottom of the leaf and placed on the rim of a glass or skewered on a toothpick and placed in the drink. Slices of pineapple, cut either in quarters, halves or eighths can also be used with the leaves.

Above: Banana slices. Below: Honeydew melon and rockmelon balls on a toothpick.

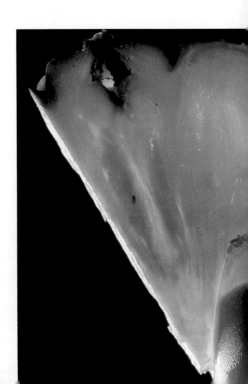

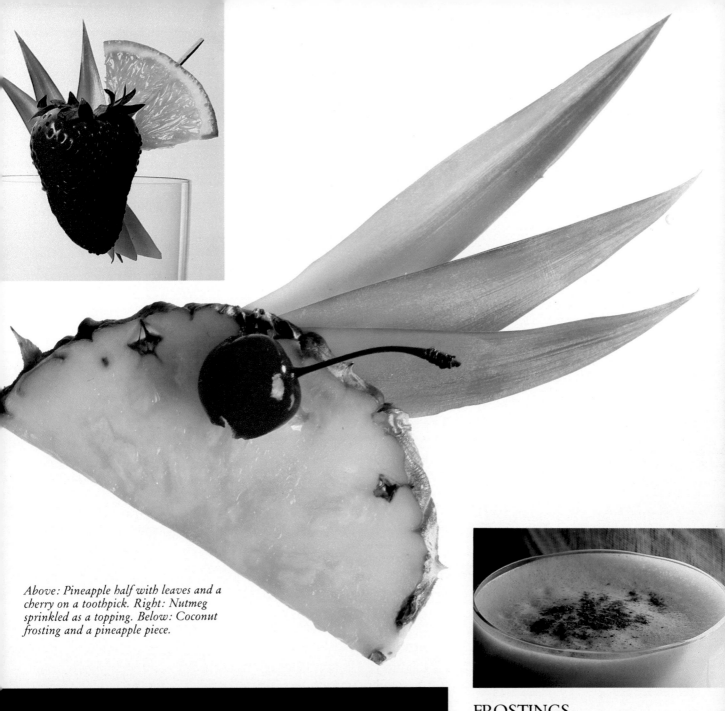

Above: Pineapple half with leaves and a cherry on a toothpick. Right: Nutmeg sprinkled as a topping. Below: Coconut frosting and a pineapple piece.

FROSTINGS

Glasses can be dipped in salt, lightly beaten egg white, sugar, coconut or instant coffee or cocoa. Remember to rub the rim with lemon or orange first. Water will just dissolve the frosting.

TOPPINGS

Freshly grated whole nutmeg, freshly ground cinnamon, freshly ground coffee beans or instant coffee, grated chocolate or chocolate curls (made by pulling the blade of a sharp knife or a vegetable peeler along a block of chocolate).

FRUIT

Many fruits are easily blended and add colour, flavour and body to drinks. Listed are the most suitable fruits for mixed drinks.

Apples: Do not blend apples, use apple juice instead.

Apricots: Firm and juicy when ripe, canned apricots are also suitable after they have been drained.

Avocados: Produce thick drinks when blended with cream.

Bananas: A strong tasting fruit, the banana must be blended until smooth. Adding créme de banane to a cocktail with fresh banana will make it sweeter.

Cherries: Canned cherries are the most suitable as they have the stones removed. Maraschino cherries are used for decorating particular cocktails.

Grapefruit: Has a tangy citrus flavour.

Lemon: Balances the sugar-level of cocktails and is best used freshly-squeezed.

Limes: Have a sweet-sour taste. Lime cordial can also be used and will sweeten a drink.

Mandarines: Very juicy fruit with a subtle flavour; segments can be used as decoration.

Mangoes: Have a very distinctive flavour and aroma. They must be very ripe and will thicken a drink. Mango nectar can be substituted but will not provide the same texture as the fresh fruit.

Melons: Add body to a drink but do not have a very strong flavour.

Oranges: Sometimes the skins are added to drinks; unsweetened juice can be substituted for freshly squeezed oranges.

Passionfruit: A very sweet fruit which can be used in blended drinks; bottled passionfruit can also be substituted.

Peaches: Must be peeled before blending, canned peaches can be used and will add a sweeter flavour to the drink.

Pears: Must be carefully handled so as not to bruise; must be peeled before blending; canned pears can be substituted.

Pineapples: A very sweet fruit that must be ripe. Canned slices can be used but are sweeter than the fresh fruit. The juice as well as the fruit is used in many cocktails.

Raspberries: Ripe fruit add colour and texture to a drink, they can be frozen and blended; raspberries will keep in the refrigerator for a few days.

Strawberries: Must be washed so as not to give a gritty taste, they add good colour and flavour.

RIGHT: Blended banana and passionfruit are ingredients of **Passion**, *page 68.*

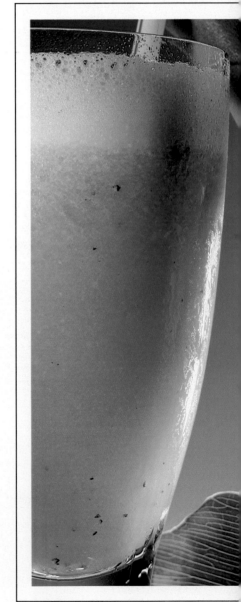

GLOSSARY

Advocaat: A Dutch liqueur made from egg yolks, sugar and brandy.

Amaretto: An Italian liqueur with an almond-apricot base.

Anisette: A very sweet colourless aniseed-flavoured liqueur.

Apricot Brandy: A highly flavoured liqueur made from apricots.

Benedictine: A sweet herb flavoured brandy-based liqueur.

Bitters: Made up of aromatics, contains roots and herbs and is used for flavour.

Blackberry Brandy: A dark liqueur flavoured with blackberries.

Blackberry liqueur: Also known as Cassis, contains blackcurrants, brandy and sugar.

Boilermaker: A shot of straight scotch followed by a beer chaser.

Bourbon: An American whisky made from grain and aged in charred oak barrels. At least 51% corn.

Brandy: Distilled from fermented juices of ripe grapes and other fruits.

Campari: An Italian aperitif with a strong bitter taste.

Champagne: A light sparkling wine, usually white and traditionally from the famous Champagne district in France.

Chartreuse: A liqueur which contains more than 130 spices and herbs. There are two types: yellow which is light, and the green which is heavier and stronger in spirit strength.

Cherry Brandy: A liqueur made from the juice of cherries and brandy.

Chianti: A dry Italian wine mostly red, but some white is available.

Cognac: Brandy from the Cognac region in France.

Cointreau: A sweet colourless liqueur with an orange flavour.

Crème de Banane: A brandy-based liqueur with a banana flavour.

Crème de Cassis: A liqueur with a blackcurrant flavour.

Crème de Cacao: A sweet dark liqueur made from cocoa beans, vanilla and spices. Has a cocoa flavour.

Crème de Fraises: A sweet liqueur with a strawberry flavour.

Crème de Framboises: A sweet liqueur with a raspberry flavour.

Crème de Menthe: A peppermint flavoured liqueur. Available in white, green or red.

Curacao: A sweet liqueur made

from wine or grape spirit, sugar and orange peel. Available in orange, white, green, and blue.

Drambuie: A liqueur based on Scotch and heather honey.

Dubonnet: A dark red aperitif wine with a slight quinine taste.

Galliano: A gold coloured liqueur with licorice and aniseed flavour.

Gin: A distillation of grain with a juniper berry flavour.

Glayva: Scottish liqueur similar to Drambuie.

Grand Marnier: A golden-brown French brandy liqueur with an orange flavour.

Grenadine: A red non-alcoholic sugar syrup used for sweetness.

Green Ginger Wine: Wine made from fruit and Jamaican ginger.

Goldwasser: A colourless sweet liqueur with gold flakes flavoured with orange and aniseed.

Kahlua: A Mexican coffee liqueur made from cocoa beans, coffee beans, vanilla and brandy.

Kirsch: A colourless fruit brandy distilled from black cherries.

Kummel: A colourless liqueur flavoured with caraway seeds and cumin.

Maraschino: A colourless Italian cherry-flavoured liqueur.

Midori: A Japanese musk melon liqueur, lime green in colour.

Ouzo: A Greek liqueur with an aniseed flavour.

Parfait Amour: A highly scented French liqueur made from lemons, oranges, brandy and herbs. Light purple in colour.

Peach Brandy: A liqueur with a peach flavour.

Pernod: A French aperitif. Pernod 45 has an aniseed flavour, Pernod Pastis has a licorice flavour.

Pimms: No 1 has a gin base. No 2 has a whisky base. No 3 has a brandy base. No 4 has a rum base. No 5 has a rye whisky base. No 6 has a vodka base.

Rum: A distillation of molasses from crushed sugar cane. Colour can vary from white to dark.

Sabra: A liqueur with a chocolate and orange flavour.

Sambuca: An Italian liqueur with a soft anisette flavour.

Southern Comfort: An American liqueur with a brandy and bourbon base and a peach flavour.

Sugar Syrup: A mixture of equal parts white sugar and water. Boil until sugar is dissolved. Can be stored in refrigerator indefinitely.

Tia Maria: A Jamaican liqueur based on rum. Has a coffee flavour.

Triple Sec: White curacao, see curacao.

Tequila: A colourless spirit made from the fermented juice of a cactus plant from Mexico, the agave or mescal.

Toddy: A mixture of spirit and hot water.

Vermouth: A wine fortified with herbs.

Vodka: A colourless and almost tasteless distillation of grain.

Wine: Usually the fermented juice of grapes.

Whisky: A distillation of grain, malt, sugar and yeast. Also Irish whiskey and rye whiskey.

LIQUEURS

There are thousands of liqueurs available throughout the world, some are fruit-based, others herb-based and others still are plant- and nut-based.

Monks and physicians were the first to mix these exotic ingredients which they originally used for healing purposes.

In the 1500s the Italians began mixing these potions and drinking them for pleasure. Fruit liqueurs resulted because much of the fruit harvested in the summer had to be preserved for winter.

Some of the more common liqueurs are listed.

FRUIT-BASED LIQUEURS

Apricot: One of the most popular fruit liqueurs, it is made from softening apricot flesh in brandy.

Banana: The best of these liqueurs have a light colour and a strong smell of ripe bananas. The most popular is Crème de Bananes, which is made from a maceration of bananas in spirit.

Blackberry: The brandy flavoured with blackberry juice has low alcoholic content and a fruity sweet taste, whereas that distilled from blackberries has a dry flavour and a high alcoholic content.

Blackcurrant: Cassis is the name given to this fruit-based liqueur which results from blackcurrants being softened in spirit (usually brandy) for about two months. When this liquid is mixed with sugar and distilled it produces Crème de Cassis.

Cherry: Cherries are pressed, the juice is extracted then mixed with brandy. Maraschino is made by crushing the cherries and stones, then distilling and sweetening the liquid.

Coconut: Formed by softening coconut flesh in white rum.

Melon: One of the new style of liqueurs, this liquid has a very sweet flavour. Midori is the widely known brand.

Orange: These liqueurs are known as curacaos and come in a variety of styles such as dry and bitter.

They are made from grape spirit, sugar and orange peel.

Peach: This liqueur is produced from peaches which are matured in brandy with other juices.

Raspberry: This soft fruit is soaked in spirit to produce Creme de Framboise. When it is distilled, a dry tasting, colourless spirit called framboise results.

Strawberry: Fraise or creme de fraise is the liqueur formed by strawberries. It is known as fraise de bois and is produced from wild strawberries.

HERB-BASED LIQUEURS

Benedictine: This very sweet liqueur has a strong herb aroma and is amber coloured. It was first made by the monks of the Benedictine monastery at Fecamp in Normandy.

Drambuie: This liqueur is based on Scotch malt whisky that has been flavoured with honey and herbs.

Galliano: An Italian liqueur with a lemon-aniseed flavour and golden colour. It is sold in tall flute-shaped bottles.

Irish Mist: Based on whisky and heather honey.

Sambuca: Witch elderbush and liquorice are the major components of this Italian liqueur. A popular way of drinking it is with three coffee beans set alight on top. This adds a toasted flavour to the drink.

PLANT AND NUT-BASED LIQUEURS

Almond: This liqueur is made from bitter almonds and the crushed stones of fruits.

Anise: One of the oldest known flavourings, anise is the base of this liqueur. It has a taste like liquorice.

Chocolate: This liqueur is flavoured with roasted cacao beans and is known as creme de cacao.

Coffee: Coffee liqueur, creme de mocca and creme de cafe are made from coffee beans which have been soaked and percolated.

Mint: These liqueurs have a tangy aroma and are made by crushing oil from the mint leaves.

INDEX